Ordinary Time

A Collection of Verses

Phillip Neal Tippin

Ordinary Time
by Phillip Neal Tippin

All poems and titles:
© 2020 by Phillip Neal Tippin. *All rights reserved.*

Cover Illustration:
Rio Colorado. Oil on Canvas. 16" x 20"
© 2020 by Jeffery Sparks. *All rights reserved.*
www.jefferysparks.com

Graphics and book design:
© 2020 by Christopher Tompkins. *All rights reserved.*

Catalog Number 009

darkly bright
press & design

www.darklybrightpress.com

Table of Contents

Folk Lyrics   11

On Local Trees   57

Turn Again   69

Ordinary Time

A Collection of Verses

Phillip Neal Tippin

for Jenae

Folk Lyrics

Irregulars

Some metaphysical folk verse,
That's all that can be mustered
From a muzzle loaded farm hand
Who'll come out to march and fight
With a furrow harnessed to his mind—
He can speak to *her* without a word.

Triumphal Entry

We planted an Oak, my daughter and I
The foal of an oak, new leafed and unsure
First light was the morn of the first of the week
Nut cracking, death buried, unleashed
Quivering stood as we patted the earth
Never yet bearing the weight of the wind
Winters of snow, summers of leaf
Rooks in the arms, blue-sky'd relief
Toes of the young feel for bend but not break
Force of the storm the lightning close breaks
Saw and teeth cleave for heat and for board
Grown men its forms, tear down to re-bore
Unburdened, our small tree untested
Growing in light of the oldest of lessons
Whose weight the elder tree did willingly bear
Whose climber clung, bare, bearing the wold.

Dawn

Dawn of night
Death black upon the brow
Blood pierces sky then pools
Settles to sobs and sinks beneath the stone
Night's the villain when light is gone

Dawn of light
Sun-laced with glory
The solace of morning
Grave sight the villain sees when leaps the day
Weeps dew for empty night not taken

The Quarry

This morning I walk forested
Beneath finch leaves, frosted pine
And desiring prospect mount
The wall of a hillside hollow
Oak rimmed and boulder mouthed
To view the bursting day.
Risen resting still among
The rocky cloister, I,
Like brothers valley'd in the abbey,
Come to quarry stones for home.

Spectre

I've been lodged with a peripheral vision
Intimation of a threat revealed,
Walking into webs, a flight and scurry,
Speck flecks a blackwing or fleetfeety thing
Appears in wood, room wall, window frames
Furtive something, neverquite seeable
Sparks a sharp turn to see the againgone.
Just aberrated eye, myself assures
But this spider, bat, gnat, eludes inspection
Or a repeated show by attention
Mocking attempts at cornea cornering.
So, by physio's sway medicate this spectre grey?
Or, as life's wing-tipp'd edge and log-lodged find
As the thorn that may convelesce my eye?

The Rupture

Lost to Sea

The dam bladder broke.
Drained in a day—
Gutted, the great bass
Flap gasping up the muck,
As aged clams drycrack
Heron and mallard drag
The turned to, the
wrenched to, stench.
—Death By Water loss.

One Month In

One month in—
The creek's intestinal lining
Stripped, the way now runs
Long life's line exposed to sun
As some swell, some shrink
Crease, coil through town like
Something the dog drug out
On which I stepped and
Lingered long among us.
Putrefying's sound is smell.

Buena Vista

Con found in me
What will not glimmer, brought from water to life
A reflected, unrefracted, fool's golden light
Oh, Great Alchemist, wrought by piercing vein
Not color only, but substance retrain
And be found of Thee.

Authority of Mountains

The authority of mountains
Might be established,
Height with might
A correlated stone's growth
Crushing thrones under weight,
Weigh wanting the rough places
Smooth the pine needle paths
Leading up the bolder slopes past
A vast vineyard, trellis splayed, as
Bent bones hold the Vine to slake
The thirst of a mounting multitude
Who gather, plow, plant, and pasture by
The wine-pressed mountain side, for,

Authority will lift again His head on high
Radiant in the descending ascent of right,
Light of such countenance, *Col de Lumiere*,
Whose Crown in burning brilliance,
Comes dazzling white to fill the sky,

And we will speak of it to one another,
This Mountain, and I will speak of it to you
And you to me, saying "Let's climb together,"
For the One who speaks as one substance
Has granted to the mountains their form
By this His Peak, their only plumb and summit.

Carthage

Oh, Lord, destroy not Carthage
What is not sin to me
Steal when I would flee
Risen spectre of such carnage
So may ripen my need
To ever plead with Thee.

Southfield

Furious winds rake the field,
Raise wraiths of white to
Lead flum'ed processions over
Snow's shadowed bier
Quaver dry as dust, ash
Ghosting the winter grey.

Didacus

San Diego's salt
Breeze-colored light makes a show / of raising the day with ease
Dappling sheen and masted silk / teem with wafted sea callings,
Over ocean at our feet / so quayed to share in time's lay
Palm frond and fray wipe morn clean / of film frought familiarity
Unresourced to write as pert / certain of West's last expanse
But as prospect spans luminous / it's filled and filtered by a
Saint's salted water

Place Setting

At culture's table
Few things are on offer
To which to give your yes, yet
Answers *all* make for deaths.
For when Yes is precedent
Presenting us with His Yes
The no's and deaths presage
Urphänomen's accepted flesh.

Transubstantiation

First from water,
Wine, a wedding
As it is in heaven—
Take it to the master of the feast.

Passes the cup—
Do whatever He tells you,

*Yet, are you able
To drink the cup that I drink?*

Himself, not passing, takes the
Sponge thrust of sour'd wine,
Vinegar, as it is on earth
To the dregs drinks our retched dry,
Then draws

His last breath.

Into Your hands I commit my spirit.
The Master of the Feast given to taste,
A pike to set a broach in the Divine
Perfectly aged, outflowing liquid life

In death.

He has done it.

Look to See

Pray to, through the One
Who looks about to see
Who touched Him, who
It pleased His Father to heal
Through Him by the faith
Of some one, the Man will look
To see and know that one
His Divinity and Humanity touched
So to delight in the Triune Love
Of this His daughter unclean
Unfit for the temple, bleeding
But as Temple bleeding came,
Touched heart, body, life to heal.
He looks to know who asks.

Infant Autumn

Nostalgia for the present presses
Missed most as the moment passes.
E'en fall's beauties rise to be blown
Before our eyes in growing lines,
Sucking the savor to hopeless avail
These golden cider ways, amber days
Timelessness smelt in a ragged wood
Smote with the dusk's crunch & curl
Lit by clear night's timorous eyes
And those of our baby brimming.
So delight, laughter lie about in piles
To rake, rake, rake, in the daylight.

Windrake

November's leave'n tide blows
In billows from the north
Eddying about the corner gate
Settling as drakes in tidal pin oak pools
While other wooded remnants scurry
With chimney smoke, past a gourded stoop
And, tumbling away down the street, retreat.

Latent Reception

Latent like music under fingers,
Poised palms over taut skin, or
A name on loosed lips.
When will it come? Press
Thunder on the heaping West, when,
As on the face of the deep, it crests.

The Awakening: An Inversion

Today I wake a schismatic.
Guilty, heretical, due burning
At the stake the selfishness,
Untenable this unity, disunity,
Drive out the slave woman
For a self-inversive vision:
The outward wasting away
The inward being renewed
Day by day, as no longer
In is in myself, now in is Christ
In you, the coinherent eschaton.
Inward a freedom to slavery,
Outward a slavery crucified.
The inner man is the New
Adam among us.

Clouded Ground

Rain from a bucket drawn
At the well of the sky
Collected at rest
To liven day
Breaks.

The Numinous

Luminous
Wakes the smokey awe of morning
Lifting by light, sounds the vale of rest
To reveal the fresh presence of being
Still

Coronado Heights

Coronado Heights is a plain parapet
Periscoping the green sea west
A Plato pattern against the sky
Yet beyond the doubt of shadow
Sacrament, its ground stands in air
Untouched but by wing and cloud—
Burst from depth of field
Here, for to be pilgrim climbed
Mounted to envisage unseen mounted west
Where the sheave waves break upon rocky slopes
Western shores sprayed of pine and cedar scent
Where storms tumble and foam the peaks
Sight of smoke and thunder, speak
Rolled and re-rolled before heading to sea
Flee unbearable might, unbearable words
Drift and whisper gently upon the hill
Mist brought near upon these rocks, this grass
Taste and see, touch and hear, lest
This hill is all you see.

Rhyme of Memory

I wish I could feel in my hands
The memory of drawn water,
Draw upon a life of the daily fact,
Task of going to the open ground,
Empty but for the dark—life rising.

Heights

Enter in
Levels of known-ness, nakedness
Beauty bathed in the eye and mind
Find paths to see from low,
Climb high

Adornment: Beauty 1
First with ornament and darkling flash
Of garment, line, flicker, glance
Shimmer and guess as of wrapping
Amongst the city, street and din, so shines
All may see, while alone intertwine by
Embrace, the marvel unraveling to glory.

Consummate: Beauty 2
Through time this adornment still clings
Yet gossamer, a golden thread too thin
To remain, light claim, falling away
For, now, two alone climb on
More beauty to find deeper in the woods and
Wild, foothills mount, meadows drink
Pools reflecting sight, delight in the eyes
Form and flow of bounded round uncoverings

Life of Love: Beauty 3
Ever after, You and I the greater beauty find
A growing transparency unspent, spreads
Unspoken ways before open, anon,
Lustrous glow, pulsing source,
Behind every veil we lift, find
Hearted here, a greater nude,
All we held worthy, wondrous—coverlet
For midst buffeting storm wind rent, shearing
Gale tears, lashes skin garments
Through the travail discarding weight even
To touch innermost cloak and open
Abreast sore climbers' rest
Upon the mountain's snow.

Love's Life: Beauty 4
Pain, story began the push
Aiming not for familiar, rather to fall,
When height upon height seem attained
Cascade into mystery of another, the other
We run yet freer in lightdrops, beauty upheld in Being
Known before time to be un-gowned between,
Source, spring, sharing, spill till with wonder
Dwell gazing upon beauty's face
Bared back to be built back upon
Every layer re-gowned in Light
Which will her lightening form
All eternity form from The Love, given
A mutual entering in of the life lying beside.

Character Spacing

Lord Jesus Christ, Son of God
Hear not by my many words
But in these one words spoken,
As thorough and slow as language
Following You, speaking to uphold.
Forgiver, heal this one borne above
To make language rise and respond,
Not over and over, but now always,
Have mercy on me, a sinner.

After Tours

The music is empire,
Headspace of statecraft
Before the citizen sea, lead
Waiting ears, eyes to arms
Seized by this priest and king
Will play the part of majesty
To a national identity, frenzy
Foreign language devouring
For one night, lights write
On the wall, drink in and die.

Philippi (Possessed of Worldly Worth)

Oh perverse generation!
My worth is my fault.

Not only a slave, one possessed,
So closely controlled I see
gods clearly, a mere mouthpiece
Yet privy to the spirit level.

Be as Balaam's ass,
This time I won't halt
Hoping for the sword fall
Divining the true Divine, I
Glimpse Heaven through hell,

Declare what I can't imagine
Speak what I can't think
Of power, some kind of channel,
Cast me out, I cannot divide

Doggedly, muster a repeated
Cry, Day after day screeching
Out of my dream. He turns, speaks,
In the name of Jesus Christ,

All worldly worth dashed
To pieces, out cast,

Dispossessed—

Infirmary

Said,
The kneeling sang
In the *infirmatory*
Until time's role
Moved all to the deadwing
Moratory's long aisle
Yet, here, the fallen wake
A story in verse
Convalescensce rolling
Eyes of the rigor caped
Mud to trees to men, awake
Rise by the hand,
"Something to eat"
Pillow propped
Receiving meal
Of bread and wine
Life's *oratory* cry
Spent.

Thanks be to God.

Familiarity

The oil slick'd sea
Is the film of liv'ed history
A Gossamer coating of death.
For the few that dive, wise daring the depths
Apocryphal return from dark sea to dark sea surface
Yet, apocalypse coming not from such descendant delving.
Rather familiar, obscured from light to dark, condescends
To the coating and reascends from the depths, not the deep.

(Soft) Naming Rights

Names do ruffle and flutter
Down from ages, across its pages.
We catch them down, each in turn
Turn to the light, lift them up.
Does the gleam match the glimmer, seams
Of the time-drenched fabrics, weave
To dress the daughter of our hearts aright?

Range

They rock upon the prairie stoop,
Stray eyes graze to a windwell
Where cattle lend necks to grass
Bent at the evening close and a sky raise'd
Glorious, recompense for the kneading
Of a wheat day's dust and an oven bake.

A Late Appearance

Contrails do stitch the daylight shut
By those silver needles thread
The criss-cross tent, hovers
A charted pattern, holding,
Loose'd then melding
Slips from the eye.

Faith Becomes Sight

Site of faith
Flare about the heavens
Oh, revelatory Light lights.
We would ride the bear
Judge the angels
Upon that Stair.

The Oak's Awakening

Serpent with a thousand heads,
Insatiate for height,
Coils up the majesty,
Year upon year, feeling
For limbs to twist to
Bind its usurpéd way,
Mete out its grip
On every twig,
As its tails teem
From darkest root
To darker work,
Clasping at the crown,
Flattering beauty
It uses to blight while
Fewer limbs in season
Bear bright and
Re-waken green, grows
The shadow of death
More spare, hard cast.
While all of this,
Every last ghastly capillary,
Consumes presence, spreads
The groan-moanings of creation's
Wind in the dying giant of an oak.

Now despite its 'during strength
To hold the rot, nothing,
Nothing in the wooded round
Can lift even a finger of will
To snap the serpine spine,
That fine wire, that creeping snare
Leaving a death-bound asphyxiate,
There, when, by the hand of man,
A few well-placed blows
Would its death asphyx.

Well, we came here, near to live
At the after-edge of another's end,
A human home passed on,
Granted us by the life of the fore
In this place, on this street, where
Those things now must be dealt
Which the fading end left unmet
When the last disease ravaged
Both his gardens to such sorrow
At loss of their keep, their gates
Inner-locked in spite of his pleas.

So to us fall bricks to sweep, clean
Stones to uncover, hedges to mend
The garden tresses trim, clothed
And in their right mind again, rest
In the spade, rake, clipper, care.

Of a morning,
Bent on these,
Our son we sent,
Axed, to cut the cord,
Of that reverséd root
Spilling, from bitter springs,
Whose delving goes ever on,
In pride, ever higher.
Yet, at its quick, such a
Fell beast may be felled
Where the scales do crease,
At the base of the tree,
At the foot of the rood
Where the worm heart lies,
Wormwood resides. So,
When comes this son
To the trunk's bind,
What all the forest
Thought not, could not
Dream to do,
He did.

Father,

Father,
Have mercy on me, a sinner
Uncharitable in action while in thought
Protected by the sham of a mental charade.
Oh, this clandestine self willing consort
Transform by a transfiguration of me
By Christ in ordinary.
Amen

Naturally

Whose song to the Babe
At her breast is prayer
To God Most High
And, also, the call of home,
Through field and street
For Him to come in,
Rings from Mary,
Mother of God.

Ingenthorn

Ingenthorn
By the shore
Sees the sun rise
But never set.
Once at my eve
Her form I knew
By the Westering
Shadow she threw.

Kombolskini

As the knotted
Crowd passes
My blind eyes
Follow with a
Beggar's cadence
Down the strand
To the end, crying
Have mercy!

—*Take heart.*

Construct

#1 David

When I want to
Build a house to
Legitimize, frame You, fame You
Build You what I built,
You, the Giver, ask "Did I?"

#2 Naaman

Nam-ed
Sent by, led by a servant,
"What did you go out to see?"
Take the Word, in sinking receive
A river like ours yet fully divine
Dipped, washed, bathed,
Baptized into the house of God
Up from the Jordan
Follows his Master in Whom
The river by washing will be cleansed

Epiphany, theophany,
Even faith of a maiden
Here preface icons writ of Your grace
Foretell greater things than this

The angels of God ascending and
Descending on the Son of Man

Now, as "your servant," come again
Wealth of nations, refuse
Give rather dirt on which
This dust may bow,
To be laid a stone in Jerusalem.
That which you tore down, raised
Build me from this soil, Bethel,
Stone of house of city of King's dom,
That we may cry on Your earth, aright.

Mystic Religion

Tyranny of the theory when no authority remains
To reprove or correct in public dogma's domain
No dictator general to remartial the lost foray
Yet mystic of the minutia has supposed remnant say
A power complete as minuscule, ruling over a
Forever half-ed kingdom as each lord races to halve their
Claim again and again to gain greatest focus, locus
From which to feel secure, untouchable until the next
Division when all is lost and self found unreliable as
A generalist when no generalized doubt allowed
Powers the parabola of bondage seen as might,
The one who fears no anarchy of the assumed
In the realm outside one's own vile, the vilest, mad monarch.

    For lording of specialization is tyranny over the
    Specialist, readily ruled by a greater mystique,
    Impulse religio, submitting to the un-know
    Of others' ken, guarding the hope aggregate
    Supersaturated, precipitate divinity of acute ignorance.

Throw off, not for the found fallacy or self referential agnostic trust,
But for the unfounded Maker, making, poeisis pointing to the more
The marvelous, giving the face of wisdom, losing the wisdom
Of the world's diviners' divining their poetry of wine is water tasted
Except that it is drawn by command, even then it is a
Carrying of the Word, whatever the ladle holds it is best, not worst
For last, He condescends to let us read, drink
Saves face, appearing in the delight of Cana

    May I also walk by obedience, rest
    In Mystery, Yet of the One
    Who walks on water, hovering.

The Miraculous Catch of Fish (Icon)

Fresh made are the fish
Which fill the net of obedience.

Obedience
In this very place
Is the day's work
After a night's failure.

To leave all claims
To others, to the Lord
Shore up no store
His Name is abundance.

In scarcity may I sit, listen,
Make repair.
In abundance flee the catch,
Follow Thee.

You have called creatures before,
A coming together too great for many
To assent, now those he'd left before
Not by two but by hundreds call
And they come, all rushing in,
Myth undone by woven nets
And by the sinking boats of *now*.

Casting for the called,
Reaping at the ripe.

The Deposition (Icon)

He left Himself hanging,

The tissue tore
As we pulled Him
Off the nails
Pale to injure
More this flesh
Outspent with
A living touch

Hands given to love,
After the end—before the beginning.

Who bore our sins
In His body, now
Borne down,
The weight of the dead

What are they holding?
What is that weight,
In the sacrament of
Bodies lifting His bloody body down?

The fluids of life and death
Matted and caked
On the walls
Of the temple
Torn down.

Rubble of Heaven

The Entombment (Icon)

The dead bury their own dead
They know the way
of things.

Yet, what to do with a body
Which never felt that internal blow.
A defaced, yet undefiled, substance?
Place below?

Plant the Seed of Jesse.

They wrapped Him in sheets as
He plumbed the nightmare of sleep.

Wrapped with the dead of Ramah,
Mothers weeping, refusing comfort,
Lying slain with the children,
With the children.

Body
Left to be cleft with us
Until the whisper, "Mary"
And we see His face.

Entrusting His flesh to them
Knowing what's in a man.

Faithful with much
By burying the gift
For a return.

The Word
Swaddled,
Let's go and see.
Made flesh
Swaddled,
Why do you seek?
Come and see!

Yet, myrrh will linger.

Transfiguration (Icon)

Don't send out to search.
You will find no one
To bury among the dead.
One must be led and then,
Only by Jacob's Ladder,
Will you go up to find
The guides conversing
With the Promise.

With the decidedly untransfigured,
A babbler on the mount,
Invited to listen
Coherently.

Tabernacle with Emmanuel
Impossible with men yet
Cephas, Ciaphus, Balaam
Request, prophesy, bless.

Unbuilt, Unfilled,
The Temple is
Spilling His Glory

Filling eyes with good things,
The whelming flood—
Precious cloud cover.

On Local Trees

Way-lane my path and of their councils climbed
Since youth they sleep and wake my eye
A breath upon, breathed on by lilt
And waver of limb-ed forest and needled height.

Sycamore

Ah, yon' sycamore would hurl
His fond-furied wrath, the wind
To loose himself, in spite
To stand bare as night
In grey starken blight,
His wreck 'round him
Flack fallen, skin, limb
Now an elbowed, gesticulate
Haunted hon-ed hibernate
Raised flay'd fingers hold
Wagnerian stricken chord.

And yet, and yet,

Lithe moments loose the great green head
Rolling with mirth of a sylvan light.
For whit of sprig and twig,
Round glad gather to hear
Tales of sprit and span
Freshness drowses draughts of spring
And stand him stately 'dorned,
To make the fury of a northern night
Seem a sprite.

White Pine

Known in fur and cone, it writes the peaceful
Bearance of quiet and cold.
A restful tree is he that sleeps and grows.

Red Bud

A beauty in bloom but brittle.

Bur Oak

The bur oak, mangled in mighty memory
Staff sticks sprout
Leafs from every crook
Bristle back and brow, as it were
Pipe smokes and branch curls
Heady cloud taps while his root fast
Hones lifelong journey, abundant
A cap o'er many an acorn son.

Cottonwood

Threads its fife upon the wind
Spinning, adrifting timbereled gin
Gentle come, such snows in summer sun.
But a soft hearted tree, giving its pledge,
May break itself upon black thunder's edge
But its memory is short and it surges forth
With claps and gold platters of joy.

Bradford Pear

Knows no small wound, this clan
Rotund, full, white sprung dressed
Or split in half.

Willow

Willow broods upon the source
Rivers lap and returns in form,
A spring welling up to pour out upon
The pond, still reflecting
Its weeping and wiping.

Locust

Grows old like stone, brine yellow
Mold of ancient shivered wood
Hung with fern, fen dripping dark
Poison pods, rattle the dirge.

American and Siberian Elm

Twins in kind, fraternal
Grown paternal across the years.
Death and war came to the elder,
The younger uncalled, uncared
For the A's spared is age and shade
For the S's undared is brokenness and shame.

Osage Orange

Hideous hide-bound hedge
Sinuous, dark, yellish hued,
Hard, haggard, un-cow'd, unkempt
Where woman and apple seem red
Here unveiled: green witch'd and worm'd.

Walnut

Green fruit, fallen husk
Charred (pia) mater, nut crust
Pale shell'd flesh
Begotten seed flesh
From strapping frame and lashing fronds fallen
He gives and gives and does not seem to take.

River Birch

A woodland writer
Poet printer joiner
Sketches poplar visions
Shaving the curling page
Press to the wold.
For, persistent his wager:
The transcendence of nature.

Turn Again

Setting Sacramental West

Eve's isle draped glorious in royal retire.
The assembled, awash, all rose resplendent
At the midair cascading stair for
The organ-ization of a sun's
Recessional ayre. I would hear,
Yet, at such a distance, could only see.

Look Away (All Saints Day)

—Look away,
Look a way off
Over the distant strain,
Shade your eyes
To the vast Light,
Before you turn—
Turn again to the stayed leagues
Of an arm's length life,
And to a lone cloud—
The span of a man's hand.

Apocalypse Songs

Advent I

Look,
   For,
      Apocalypse to the dark night came
         Stoled among the beasts of burden
            Groaning hills blushed by the song
              Of His Advent rending
            Skies, coming down
               Silent as Light.

Advent II

                      Adam,
               Milton's Michael
           To him pre-vision given
         Of the tide to rise to reach
       The mark of the dark, grown darker
     yet still darker as forerunner announces
    Epoc-alypse upon the race and deep waters
  Flood-tide to match the fell spot despoiled, woe to
                      All
                Noah new
          Bearer of the prophecy
         To begin again at dawn light
        To cut a path to night o'er time's
      flight began rain bowed, morning vowed
   Runs again a course till gathered clouds, ominous,
Unable to burst, promise upholding, yet darken so darkens
The night of advent's march till voice of one calling "make straight"
For He, death black'd by swallowed death wracked, will make smooth,
All pairs call, the cataclysm impending and eu-catastrophic fury to break upon
                      Him

Advent III (Benedictus)

Father of time, aright
Living Your advent is story, song
Life in context formed, forming
For and aft running
Jeremiah's Stone and Jonah's Vine
Four hundred years and nine months
But my mouth shut
'Til birth and "John" writ
Fulfilled, placed in time
Posture of worship in the wings
For at the apocalypse
Christ waits, the path of night
No speed, wrapped Himself thus
Swaddled in story
Things worth saying,
Time taking,
Time hearing,
And the we
Still midst the rhyme,
Benedictus Dominus Deus
Repeat the sounding joy
Of the dawn breaking
Time meeting
Now.

Advent IV (Magnificat)

Apocalypse of life
Leaping heard
When dark to Vanta
Pin pierce, reversed prism
Spun colors of promise
To first light, glory, mandorla
Of fullness, one substance
Meiosis, death inversing
Magnificent to the small,
Poor, body and soul,
Lifts lowly by low
Fills hungry by hunger
Scatters proud by Seed
He blooms, Aaron's staff
Flowers *and* fruit
The flutter and beat of God
In womb wound
Stabled by heart and lung
Knit, the Incarnation
Stirs in Mary, mother of God

Polyphony

Epiphany of our Lord
Light of revelation to the gentiles
Radiance as of jasper
So far-sons seek
Dwelling fullness bodily
Idolatry-consuming Substance
In the worship of idolaters, unadulterated
Image and temple of the Immortal
"King and God and sacrifice."
Kings of the earth go in and out
Of The Holy City come down
Bearing gifts, their glory, polyphony

Epiphany

Language comes true as lights in the night.
Now follow *through*. Obey the sight.
Eye and body make reply.

Terce (Epiphany III)

In the erstwhile
By the swine sty
Cold charred arms of hedge
Treeline the frozen slop—
  a distant land
Yet of near approach
To where the Brother
Provides the wine—for,
It is the feast of Cana
It is the time of gifts.

Ordinary Time I

Rippled leaves lapping light
Whisp of a whirled wind
Play elven games with my sight.
Yet if I will hear with ears
And not with my eyes
Whorled limbs whisper:
The tides of the wind
Only answer by
The tides of a mind
Going out to see.

Ordinary Time II

You said "watch therefore"
Yet all ten virgins slept
& I sleep while You wept.
Speak, awake my sleep
Grant Spirit of willing
And flesh of the meek.
"Your name is oil poured out" spilling
For the widow's son am I
Who eats and drinks to die
Light of Your countenance, be mine!

Ordinary Time III

Custom grown with cars on roads crossing fields
Natural as cattle, wheat, wheels but one example,
Material might become commonified and the otherness behind lost
Lost on me. For, the conspirings we make in reflecting Image
Sedate, subdue, obscure from which I behold and behold.

Yet, a morning light across the highway
Paints alienate ships in flicker and flash,
Separates from anything that grows
Can grow, or looks to grow. Finally,
A curtain crease in my norm
Through the elements of which
I feign to write of, consider much
Densified dross, single vision, mass voidance,
Suddenly parts, allows a step behind
To the otherness of original other,
The being upheld, she wakes in a garden.

The Triad Bell

Chaos of sound tuned to self surrounds
The throng that flocks the streets and halls
Over the clambering heap whistles wind
Cast about by engine noise, the consummit

Tintinnabulum

Turn again, the stone gate
By the door enter, enfold as
The Eucharistic bell tolls
In the silence hear again

Take the note, the Triad
This our returning, our call
Home, so rung that
His life may dance upon the air,
Over ripened fields, strike again

That quickening tone
Which rings out harmonic
Through the week, ours
Arvo's Pärt to play,
To tune the time
To bear Christ's death
In the heart, ear, stomach, carry
Take the piercing,
Rung hammer's knell, the new
Note to key all registers true,
Hear again

Clear chimes from the abbey's hill
Roll, so, return to, listen at
Our shard dome, recast
From the spire heart calling
Struck, stricken, silent
The real presence,
Sounds the fallen falling
Fathoms reverberate
The overture and hum of His resounding
And again by its ringing may sing.
Now strike again.

The Temptation

He has filled the hungry with good things

Revers'ed weakness,
At theopportune moment
Attack, look of hunger
The deceiver deceived
By signs of weakness
Which are His strength.
May I too appear prone
In His hunger follow
By fasting readier cling
When the wicked wings sing.

From Where I Sit (Holy Week)

From where I sit
I can see the spot
The Chisholm banks down,
Across the Sand, and up
Following this prairie cut
The cattle wheels carved
Two lines to pre-furrow
A land rutted through.

Liturgical whiplash
Gives the blade its purchase
As it overturns the bedded
Soil of heart and mind, plows
From fasts to palms to lashes
And makes another pass across
A time rutted through.

I sit resting from unearthing
Stones laid and 'scaped
With care mere years ago,
Now, solid with silt. Oh,
Such little mark and
Scuff shall I leave,
Regardless of how
Tight my turnings
And patterning ways,
I trod the human scope as
Ever a prairie over grows—

  But for the turning of *the* year,
  But for west then east facing—

He said to me,
Get in the way of the gospel, so
Station fallow self in Your furrow
To be rutted through.

Easter Vigil

"He descended into hell"

I woke to a blast on Holy Easter Eve
Storm of peril and fright above
About my bed had broke
And thinking thus upon the day
My heart lay with Him and them, the dead
Beneath the tumbling boulders of fire
Tearing the underworld with winded blind
Lost long from song-ed stars of sight
When breaking, splitting voice racks
The roll round, and rolls on
Rends the night, livid scene
Wake with hail, Harrowing hell
Holy storm had sown in thorn
Reap a blazen Horn, Almighty
Pelting power with substance, replete
Thus they spring, quaking
Rise from bedded death
For the Seed of the woman buried
Kernel and cultivator one, calls
Brings His reward with Him
Flings torrent and fire and ice at night
The Water and Seen and Seed of life
In me, a soil, and in the soils beneath
He gathers the dust dead hearts and
The dead-living to form the risen
On Paschal Morn

The storm passed, passage
Across the sky with awe
And final rumble echoes expanse
Wide roaming sound as if stone
Were opening to the Dawn

"May I rise with You, the Morning."
Then I slept.

Ascension & Pentecost

Up as a place
He condescends
By which forms
Meet fulfillment.

Back as a place
Kingdom ascent
On which Fire
And Might open.

Hearing (Pentecost)

Preoccupied with the words of every language,
Complete resourcefulness of the Paraclete,
Replete when the spoken gift reaches open ears,
For the miracle is in the ear of the beholder,
From the words of the works of God
Comes the towering coherence of all—
—fruitfully multiplied,
Filling the East.

My love, speak these.

Trinity Sunday

I approach, as if art, to contemplate.
A riotous act and consumptive at
The labyrinthine peril of approximate.
In right headedness turn rather to right
Contemplation's sabbath rest. Theophany,
The vision's fruitfulness is Itself,
Granted as livened by trifundity.
To form from as all reality is of,
Not to find out but to find in
Not applying to but rather applying on.
In the divine nature to participate,
Grace, love, fellowship where
Thinking find themselves thought
In His love found out, led on,
Caught up, not cast back, out
We approach, in His art, to gather.

Corpus Christi

This sabbath
We awake
In medias res
Et fine

Have you never read on this day
David and his men
Ate the bread of the presence
Unlawfully enlivened?
Yet, Ahimelech will die
For sabbath rest and life
Sustained, portending the sword
And the Lord of the sabbath

When once upon the way
His disciples, being hungry,
Took grain, unscythed,
Gifted margin of life
In the Neighbor's field.
Yet, present: Temple,
High Priest, David's Lord,
Bread of the Presence,
Sabbath's end and means
For His companions to take
And crush and be filled
Since

Unslaved, from the gods of production
Masters of labor in fear of unshown
Might, dominion, power, place, lord
Upheld by work of slave, not son
Brick weight, sickle stroke,
Now these called to cease
Come out, by way of the sea
The Lord of the harvest leads
That they may rest as You rest
Not as means of production
Recharging, but as ends discharged

Whence the seventh day,
Remember, re-enact
The made-well goodness,
The peace of being upheld,
Completed. Alien, slave,
Son, daughter, your
Sabbath, not a means
But the end, to play
In the Giver's rest

Now is then, when
Uncollected, unspoilt
Living manna comes down
Our sabbath feast, provided
The Incarnation for man
Not man for sabbath

So heal
Even if in your anger,
Son of David
Make me, the Pharisee,
See

The oxen,
Shriveled hand
Are we

Stretch out,
Take, eat
Corpus Christi

The Long Wake (Facing East)

We are in
The wake of the dead
'Til morning, sit
By those laid—wait
To join the stirring,
To join their waking
To breakfast together.

(Septuagesima)

About the Poet

Phillip Neal Tippin lives with his wife and four children on the banks of the Sand Creek in Newton, Kansas, an old railroad town on the Chisholm Trail. It is a prairie place, bounded by wheat fields and flint hills. Along with pursuing his vocation as a dentist, he writes and reads among growing things. Tending to culture at the human scale occupies what margin remains.

www.ingramcontent.com/pod-product-compliance
Lightning Source LLC
Chambersburg PA
CBHW060620080526
44585CB00013B/921